I0004152

3Kiddos Publishing
ESD K9 Estie Activity and Coloring Book

Copyright 2024 By: Laura Grantham
Chelsey Lynne Lillge, The Italic Illustrator

Distributed In Partnership With
3Kiddos Publishing

All Rights Reserved, Including the right to reproduce this book or
portions there of in form.

www.3kiddospublishing.com

ISBN:
979-8-9898171-5-3

Hi! My name is Estie!

I am an electronic storage device detection K9.

I love making new friends! I call all my friends "Estie's Besties."

We will have fun together as we learn internet safety just by doing my puzzles and activities inside my book.

DOGGLE

K9 Estie's Besties Online Saftey Pledge

🐾 I will tell my trusted adult if anything makes me feel sad, scared, or confused.

🐾 I will ask my trusted adult before sharing information like my name, address, school name, phone number, and personal photos.

🐾 I will not meet face-to-face with anyone I "met" online.

🐾 I will talk to my trusted adult if I believe a friend is in danger or is being cyber-bullied.

🐾 I will be a good online citizen and not do anything that hurts other people or is against the law.

As one of Estie's Besties
I promise to ALWAYS stay safe online:

MY NAME: _____

MY SIGNATURE: _____

TODAY'S DATE: _____

K9 Estie

OLCEIP

_ _ _ _ _ _

EARTT

_ _ _ _ _

HOPNE

_ _ _ _ _

SIETE

_ _ _ _ _

SFYEAT

_ _ _ _ _ _

BYCER

_ _ _ _ _

Can you Help K9 Estie

Unscramble

the words?

Can you help K9 Estie find her treats?

Help K9 Estie
Find the 2 phones that are the same.

Circle the two phones that match.

Help K9 Estie Find all the Pairs

Draw a line connecting the matching phones

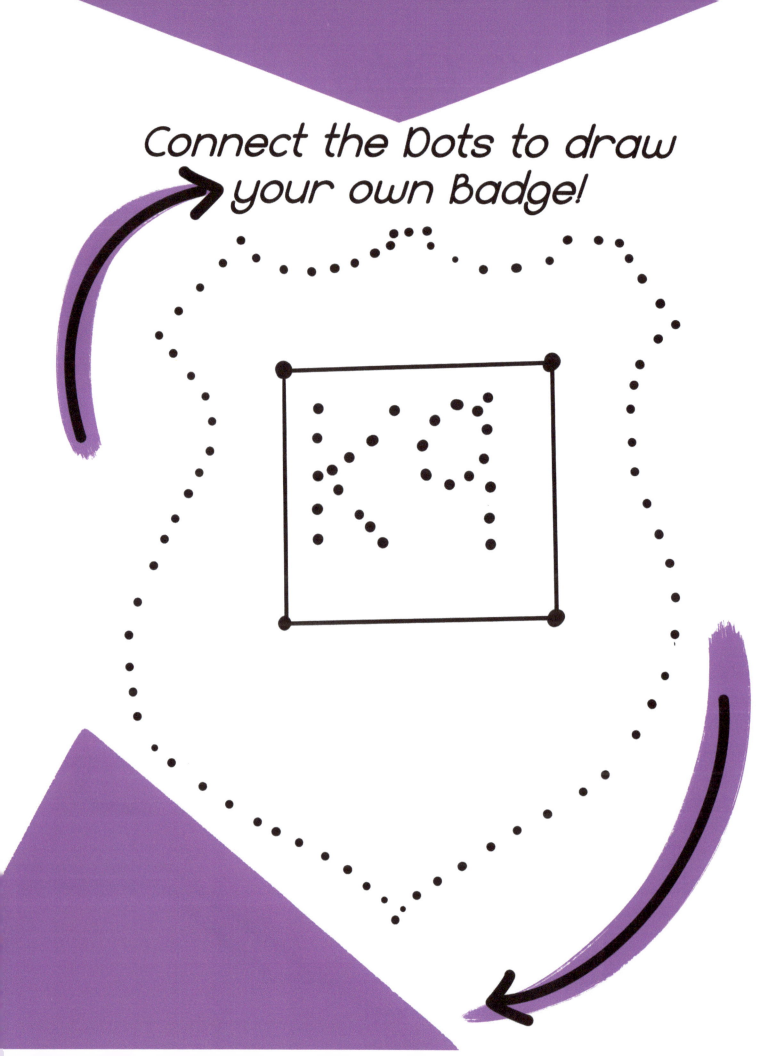

Connect the Dots to draw your own Badge!

Can You Find all 5 Differences?

Can You Help K9 Estie Get the Cellphone?

K9 Estie's Besties
Be Safe
Online Board Game

GAME INSTRUCTIONS:

Place the game piece of choice on START for each player. Each player takes turns rolling a die. The players move their game pieces the number of spaces shown on the die. Once you land on a space, read it and move game pieces as directed.

GAME PIECES:

CUT OUT GAME PIECES FOR EACH PLAYER

END

YOU REPORT A CASE OF CYBERBULLYING ON SOCIAL MEDIA
MOVE FORWARD 1 SPACE

SD

DANGER! YOU GAVE AN UNKNOWN PERSON YOUR TELEPHONE NUMBER
MOVE BACK 1 SPACE

YOU BLOCK A STRANGER ONLINE
MOVE FORWARD 1 SPACE

DANGER! YOU ARE CONSIDERING MEETING AN UNKNOWN PERSON IN REAL LIFE
MOVE BACK TO START

YOU ONLY GO TO WEBSITES THAT YOU HAVE PERMISSION BY YOUR PARENTS TO VISIT
MOVE FORWARD 1 SPACE

YOU SAW SOMETHING THAT MADE YOU UNCOMFORTABLE AND YOU TOLD AN ADULT
MOVE FORWARD 3 SPACES

YOU POSTED A FUNNY PICTURE OF A FRIEND WITHOUT THEIR PERMISSION
DANGER! MOVE BACK 1 SPACE

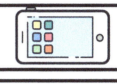

YOU SEE A FRIEND BEING BULLIED ONLINE - YOU TELL A TEACHER
MOVE FORWARD 2 SPACES

YOU POSTED A BATHING SUIT PHOTO AS PUBLIC
DANGER! MOVE BACK TO START

YOU TOOK ESTIE'S BESTIES PLEDGE TO BE SAFE ONLINE
MOVE FORWARD 1 SPACE

START

Help K9 Estie Sort and Count the Evidence?

Circle and count all of the Flash Drives and Cellphones

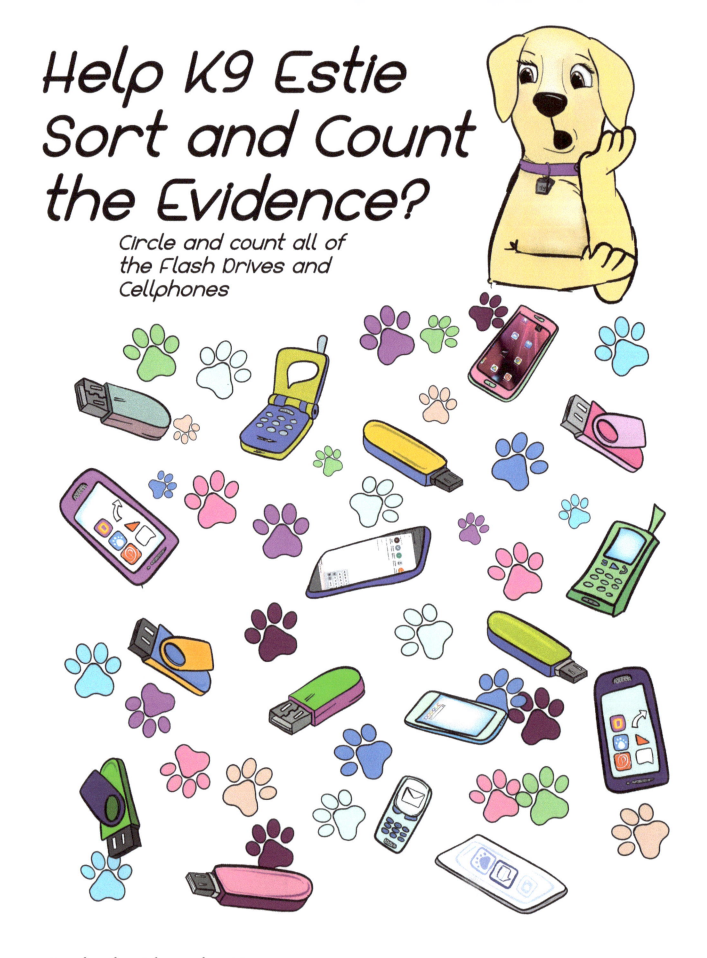

Total Flash Drives :
Total Cell Phones :

DOGGLE

Can you help Estie

Find all the technology?

Stay Classic

```
E S T I E S M F R I E N D S A
Z A K S A S A K N T V E S W X
E Z Z D Q H S Y S K J S N S D
N Z T A N E H H E X J T T B Q
M A S T O R A Z H T S I Q S M
U G T A Z I J E M Q R E R O A
C Z O H G F H P R Q I S A C V
E Q R X J F F D N L T B P I K
D L A P T O P D Q R M E O A U
F G G F Z H O V L I E S N L Q
R K E T Y A W R W N I T L M Z
C Y B E R B U L L Y M I I E W
A V C E L L P H O N E E N D H
W V D C O M P U T E R S E I Q
X U A G S A F E T Y D K V A O
```

ESTIES BESTIES   SOCIAL MEDIA   CYBERBULL

CELLPHONE   STORAGE   COMPUTER

FRIENDS   SHERIFF   SAFETY

LAPTOP   ONLINE   ESTIE

DATA

Can You Help Estie Find All of the Online Words?

Can You Help Estie Collect All the Evidence?

Circle All the Electronic Storage Devices

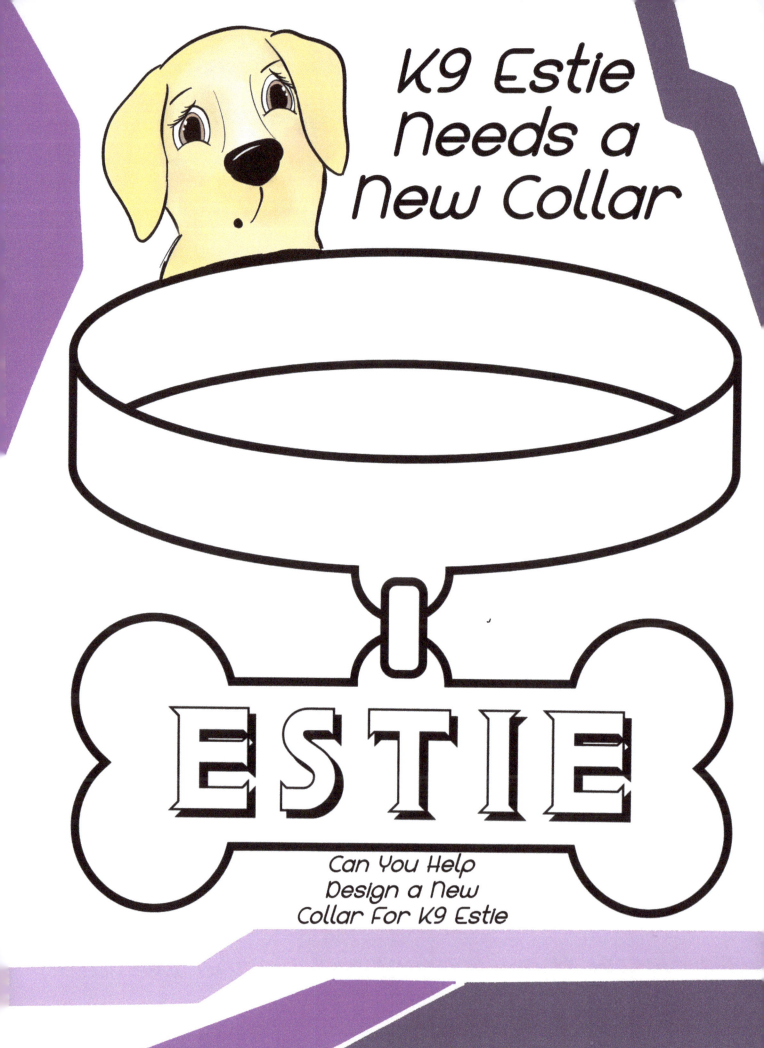

Can you Help K9 Estie with the Online Safety Puzzle?

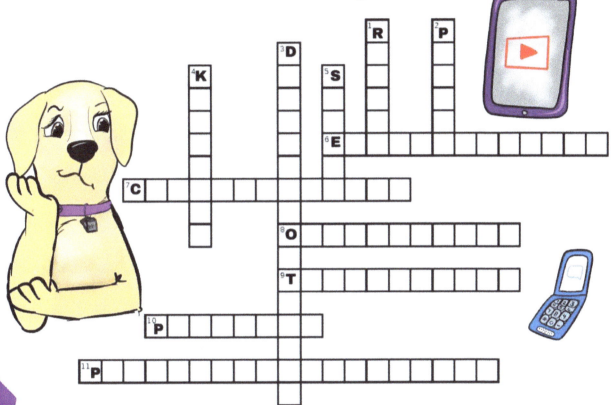

DOWN:

1. Tell a trusted adult about inappropriate online content
2. Items made by using a camera
3. Trail of data you leave on the internet
4. Having a friendly, considerate nature
5. Protection from harm
6. Friends of ESD K9 Estie who pledge to safe online

ACROSS:

7. The use of technology to harass, threaten, embarrass, or target another person
8. Sharing too much information
9. Honest, reliable, loyal
10. Secret code word to protect your information
11. Information identifying a person

WORD BANK

KINDNESS   DIGITAL FOOTPRINT   CYBERBULLYING   ESTIES BESTIES

PASSWORD   OVERSHARING   PHOTOS   TRUSTWORTHY

SAFETY   REPORT   PERSONAL INFORMATION

Help K9 Estie Match the Paw Prints

Draw a line to each matching paw.

Connect the numbers to draw K9 Estie

Which K9 Estie is Different?

TIPS FOR STAYING SAFE ONLINE

Work with your "patrol partners" (parents or guardians) to explore the internet safely.

"Investigate" websites and apps together with grown-up "sleuths" to make sure they're safe for you.

If you see something suspicious or uncomfortable online, "alert the authorities" (your parents) immediately.

"Arrest" your personal information by keeping it private and not sharing it with strangers.

Only communicate with people you "know on the beat" (friends and family) when online.

"Synchronize" your online activities with your parents' guidance to ensure a safe experience.

Remember, your parents are your best 'safety squad' online, so always seek their guidance and support.

www.ingramcontent.com/pod-product-compliance
Lightning Source LLC
LaVergne TN
LVHW061923050326

832903LV00037B/4830